Kids' Travel Guide
Paris Museums

 **Presents:**

Kids' Travel Guide
Paris Museums

Writer: **Shira Halperin**

Editor: **Yael Ornan**

Designer: Keren Amram

Cover Designer: Francesca Guido

Illustrator: Liat Aluf

Translator: Oren Amir

Translation editor: Yael Valier

Photographs: **Shira** Halperin, **Hadar** Ben Gal

Visit us: www.theflyingkids.com

Contact us: leonardo@theflyingkids.com

ISBN: 978-1499677782

Production:

www.notssa.com

Table of Contents

This is the only page for parents in this book...

Dear parents,

If you have bought this book, you're probably planning a family trip to Paris. Whether you are museum lovers or not, you are probably wondering whether to include museum visits in this trip or whether to wait until the kids are older. If you have decided to include museum trips, then this is the book for you, and if you are still debating, then this is the book for you!

You are spending a lot of time and money on a trip to Paris in the hopes that this family vacation will be pleasant and fun and will always be remembered as a very special experience.
Of course, you would be happy for your children to get to know the city - a little of its geography, a little local history, culture, customs, and what about the museums?

Paris is known for its famous museums and a visit to these museums is compulsory, even for those who don't habitually visit museums. Wouldn't you like to visit some of the most interesting museums in the world? Wouldn't you like your children to be exposed to and interested in them? And you would certainly like your children to learn a little, to enjoy themselves, to be impressed and to remember this unique experience for a long time.

The reality is often quite different. Parents find themselves frustrated as they struggle to convince their kids to join them for a museum trip. And during the museum visit, parents want to enjoy the visit but the kids are impatient. The children are not familiar with and do not understand what they are seeing, and everyone's frustration grows.

That is the reason the Kids' Travel Guide series was born.

With the Travel Diary for the Young Explorer, children become active young detectives during museum visits. In an experiential and interesting way, they learn about the world of art and museums: different styles of art, materials that artists use and interesting information on some of the leading art museums in Paris, and on the children's science museum. The children become curious learners and also become active partners in the experience, and you turn into satisfied, proud parents.

What's in the book?

The Travel Diary for Young Explorers prepares children for museum visits and exposes them in an interesting, experiential way to the world of art (but not just art), at a level suited to their age.

In the first part of The **Kids' Travel Guide - Paris Museums**, your children will be exposed to the world of museums and art — they will read fascinating snippets on the different kinds of museums in Paris, will be exposed to the main styles of art, and will receive tips that will help them discover which pieces of art belong to which style. They will also learn about different materials used by artists and when to use what material.

The second part of The **Kids' Travel Guide - Paris Museums** is dedicated to four main art museums: The Musée D'Orsay, The Musée Picasso, The Musée Rodin, and, of course, the large and impressive Louvre. And there is a special chapter on the children's science museum. Not just art...

All this is designed to encourage your children to experiment, to be active and, of course, to internalize information and experiences during the trip and afterwards, and maybe you, the parents, will learn something too.

Additionally, parts of the book are dedicated to descriptions and summaries of the visit, to the Most Beautiful Piece of Art competition (the family votes on who gets first place), and more.

Are you ready for a new experience?

HAVE A PLEASANT TRIP!

Hi Kids,

If you are reading this book,
you must be very lucky — you're traveling to Paris!

Are you excited?

Paris is a beautiful and special city with amazing places for kids and the whole family to visit. Have you heard of the **Eiffel Tower**? The **Champs-Elysées**? The Cathedral of **Notre Dame**? How about the Louvre and the **Picasso Museum**? Have you heard of those?

Paris is the city of museums! There are a lot of art museums there, and also a special museum for kids called "The Museum of Science and Industry." The art museums are always interesting — the buildings themselves are unique and fascinating and so are the pieces of art within them! And in the science museum, you'll learn about all sorts of different things.

Have you ever visited a museum? _____

If you have, which museum and where? _____

_____

Everybody knows that kids don't always enjoy art museums and they don't always have so much patience for the visit. That's normal and ok. Usually, this is because kids don't know the secrets behind the unique pieces they are looking at.

If your parents are planning museum visits during your stay in Paris, you can start getting excited - it's going to be special and fascinating and you're going to understand everything that's going on!

Before anything else, meet Leonardo. He will be your personal guide during all your museum visits. Leonardo has visited many museums in Paris and in the whole world, and he'll tell you everything you need to know and more!

If you read what Leonardo has prepared for you before you visit museums, you are guaranteed a unique experience: You are going to impress your family with your expertise in art (things that they don't even know), you're going to enjoy the games and action items (Yes, right in the middle of the museum!) and you're going to come out of it all with a great story to tell.

Who says museums are boring ⊙⊙ ?

Paste a picture of the whole
family here

Museums in Paris

Paris is the city of museums. It has more than 100 different museums.

What is a museum anyway?

A museum is a gathering place for collections of items which fit into particular categories — and there is a huge range of categories. Most importantly, you're allowed, and encouraged, to go visit and to see everything on show.

Most people think of art museums, but a museum is not only for art. There are different collections and different museums which exhibit all sorts of things.

Leonardo has made a list of different museums in Paris for you. Try to guess which of them is really a Paris museum and which Leonardo has made up ∂̊ :

- The Museum of Fashion and Textiles
- The Museum of Natural Science
- The Sewage Museum
- The Museum of the Opera
- The Army Museum
- The Discovery Museum

With this in mind, some of the most famous art museums and some of the most important pieces of art in the world are in Paris. You can stay for a week in Paris, visiting museums from morning until evening, and still not see them all ⁰̥⁰ .

Are you ready for a new experience?

What is an art museum?

An art museum is a building where works of art are collected and presented. In some cases the exhibits change from time to time, and sometimes there are exhibits that appear permanently in the museum.

Before we start, Leonardo will equip you with a few terms and concepts from the world of art so that you will be in the picture.

There are artists who create using brushes and those that use pencils and charcoal. There are those who paint people and animals and those that paint the landscape. There are artists who paint clear, understandable shapes and those who paint things that are a little hard to understand sometimes.

What kinds of materials did the artists use?

As you have seen, you can paint with all kinds of materials, with different types of painting tools and different painting methods. Here are some commonly used methods. When you walk around in the museum you can guess which materials the artists used:

Oil Paint - made from pure paint mixed with oil. Usually, artists paint on canvas or sailcloth stretched out on a wooden frame, or they paint directly onto a wooden board.

Water Color - Paint that easily dissolves in water and creates a delicate transparent look on paper. The artist begins marking the paper with faint lines of diluted paint. As the painting progresses, the artist slowly adds more layers of less diluted color. The painting is created with very soft fibred brushes, called sable brushes, or with brushes with synthetic fibres.

Drawing – Drawings are usually made from pencils or ink.

How do artists paint?

Most paintings were painted with a brush. Expensive, professional brushes are made with horse tail hair or from the bristles of other animals, but, nowadays, most brushes are made of synthetic fibres. There are many types of brushes in different shapes and sizes which are used for all sorts of purposes.

Help Leonardo connect each type of brush to the right painting.

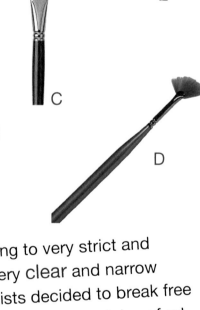

A

B

C

D

1. A brush which allows you to paint small, delicate details with great control. Hint: A round brush with a pointed tip.
2. A brush which is good for painting broad surfaces and allows you to paint with wide brushstrokes. Hint: A flat brush.
3. A brush made for painting accurate arcs and water drop shapes and for painting broad surfaces. Hint: A flat brush with a rounded tip.
4. A brush made for painting narrow, closely spaced parallel lines and excellent for painting hair and plant life. Hint: A fan shaped brush.

Many years ago artists used to paint according to very strict and exact methods. In other words, artists had very clear and narrow rules about how to paint. As time passed artists decided to break free of the rules and to create new methods. This is how new styles of art, called modern art, developed.

To help you to keep things a little straight, here is a description of some styles, or as the adults call it, movements in art.

Answers: 1-A, 2-C, 3-B, 4-D

Impressionism

Impressionist artists painted things connected with their lives, to describe the period that they lived in. They painted outside and not just in the studio. They were interested in seeing how the light affected their paintings. They used short brush strokes together with strong colors, and did not emphasize the details, so that it looked like the artist hadn't finished the painting.

Short brushstrokes

Here is an example of a painting from the Impressionism movement. It was painted by the artist Camille Pissaro in 1897
and is called "Montmartre Boulevard"

Mark the picture with arrows to show where you can find characteristics of Impressionist painting and indicate which ones they are.

Expressionism

Expressionism is an art movement in which **artists express** their **feelings**. Because artists feel or interpret what they see differently, their paintings show how they felt about the subject. For example, if the artists feel pain or hurt, they will show it through the paintings and forms that they choose.

Here is an example of a painting from the Expressionist movement. It was painted by the artist Franz Marc in 1912 and is called "The Yellow Cow"

Can you guess what the artist was feeling?

Imagine that you are an Expressionist artist and try to paint what you feel about your trip to Paris and the sites you have visited.

Abstract Art

Abstract art is created by combining shapes, lines and colors that are unlike real people or objects (like those we see everyday). They are created by the artist.

Here is an example of an abstract painting by the artist **Wassily Kandinsky**.

Did you know?
Wassily Kandinsky was not only a gifted artist but also a musician and lecturer at the law faculty of the University of Moscow.

Guess which one of these three paintings was not painted by Kandisnky and is not considered abstract art?

1

2

3

Portrait

A portrait is a painting of someone's face. Many artists paint pictures of themselves. This is called a self-portrait. The viewer can look at a self-portrait and try to guess what the artist was feeling (Was he happy or angry...).

Here is an example of a self-portrait by Van-Gogh.

Try to paint a portrait of one of your family members. How did it turn out? 😊

Leonardo has collected information about **four recommended museums** for you:
1. **D'Orsay museum**
2. **Picasso museum**
3. **Rodin museum**
4. Louvre museum

d'Orsay Museum

The date on which we visited the museum:

_____

The d'Orsay museum is a good example of a museum that is worthwhile to visit not only for the artwork displayed there, but also for the **building itself.**
Can you guess what the building was used for before it became a museum?

A hint - The building is located in a very central location in Paris.

The museum displays art from the 1800s, and you can see **paintings and statues from very famous artists** such as Monet, Gauguin, Rodin and Delacroix among others. Most of the art here is from the Impressionist movement.

Where is the museum located?

_____

Describe the building - How does it look from the outside?

_____

How does it look on the inside?

_____

Which three pictures or statues did you like the most?

_____

answer: The building was used as a train station

Picasso Museum

The date on which we visited the museum:

_____

Who said: "Give me
a museum and I'll fill it?"
That's right, Pablo Picasso.

Who was Pablo Picasso?

Picasso was one of the most famous artists in the history of modern art. He was born in Spain in 1881 and died at age 92. He painted in the modern art style.

Did you know?
Picasso's full name was Pablo Diego José Francisco de Paula Juan Nepomuceno María de los Remedios Cipriano de la Santísima Trinidad Clito Ruiz y Picasso. Let's hear you say it in one breath…

Each artist - painter or sculptor - usually has an identifiable style. So that if you know some of an artist's works really well, you can recognize his or her other works when you see them.

Picasso was an artist who worked in many different styles. When you walk through the museum you will see works that sometimes look like a different artist made them. The different styles are connected to events in Picasso's life.

For example, when Picasso was 20, a close friend of his died. He was very sad and for three years painted only sad blue pictures. Several years later Picasso met a nice woman and fell in love with her. During that time all his paintings were in cheerful shades of pink, and he painted happy scenes such as circuses.

Here are some more periods in the life of Picasso. Walk around in the museum and try to guess to what period each picture belongs:

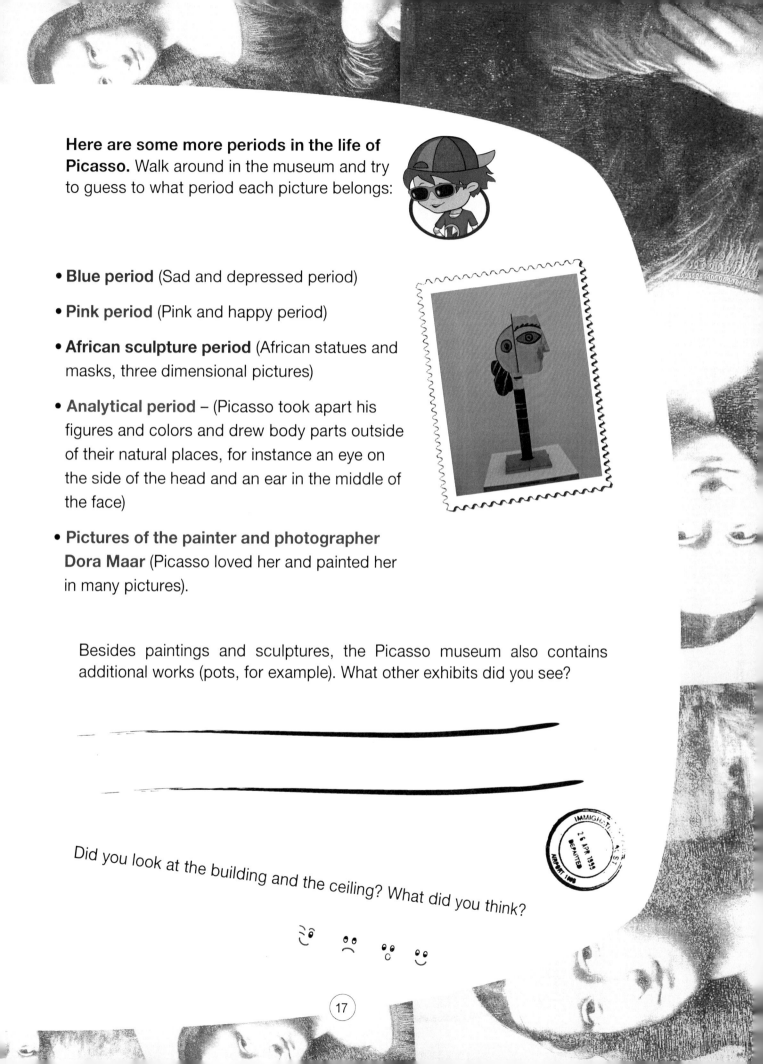

- **Blue period** (Sad and depressed period)

- **Pink period** (Pink and happy period)

- **African sculpture period** (African statues and masks, three dimensional pictures)

- **Analytical period** – (Picasso took apart his figures and colors and drew body parts outside of their natural places, for instance an eye on the side of the head and an ear in the middle of the face)

- **Pictures of the painter and photographer Dora Maar** (Picasso loved her and painted her in many pictures).

Besides paintings and sculptures, the Picasso museum also contains additional works (pots, for example). What other exhibits did you see?

Did you look at the building and the ceiling? What did you think?

Rodin Museum

The date on which we visited the museum:

_____

You won't find any pictures in the Rodin museum 😮 .
Auguste Rodin was a sculptor who mainly sculpted **figures** of people. The museum is in a beautiful building that used to belong to Rodin himself, and in which he made most of the sculptures that you will see. If you are worried that you won't have the patience to look at the statues in the museum, you should know that the Rodin museum has one big **bonus** (in addition to the stunning statues) - it is surrounded by a beautiful garden and lots of open space where you can **play**, **run** around and **meet children** from other countries.

Who was Auguste Rodin?

Auguste Rodin was born in 1840 to a very poor family. He worked as a carver in order to make a living. Only after 20 years, under the inspiration of the statues of Michelangelo, he created the sculpture called "The Age of Bronze." The sculpture looked so much like a real man that **people were sure that he had used the body of a real man to create the statue** 😊 .

Tip!

On some of the days of the week there is a sculpture workshop for kids. You can look at Rodin's work and try to make a statue like his.

"The Thinker" is Rodin's most famous statue, and it can be found in several places around the world. Although there are several "The Thinker" statues, many of them are considered authentic.

How did Rodin make most of his statues?
Rodin used the technique of casting his statues into molds. He prepared the mold in the form of the statue that he wanted to cast, and for the casting itself he used a metal called bronze.
When bronze is heated it becomes flexible and liquid, and it can be poured into a mold. Guess what happens to bronze when it cools?
That's right, it hardens and becomes a statue.
Of course the mold can be reused to create more statues.
Now do you understand why many of Rodin's statues of look exactly the same?

Where is the museum located?

_____

Describe the building - How does it look from the outside?

_____

How does it look on the inside?

_____

Which three pictures or statues did you like the most?

_____

The Louvre Museum

The Louvre is one of the most famous museums in the world, if not the most famous. Almost everyone who gets to Paris wants to **visit the Louvre**, and in fact millions of tourists visit the Louvre every year.

Did you know?
In the past the building was used as a fort and defended the city walls. After that it was used as a palace by the kings of France and in 1793 the building was opened to the public as an art museum.

The Louvre is a **huge** building. It is said that you could walk around for a full week and still not see the whole thing. As you walk around in the Louvre, you will see that the building itself is no less impressive than the art that is displayed in it (Look at the ceiling and walls.)
When you stand at the entrance, you can see that the building is divided into three wings. Each wing has a name: to the right is the Denon wing, to the left is the Richelieu wing and in front of you is the Sully wing. And **what is standing in the middle of the square?**

What can you see in the Louvre?

The museum contains a huge collection of antiquities from many different periods, cultures and countries: Greece, Rome, Egypt, the Near East the Far East and others. In addition there are statues and paintings made by many famous artists.

Most of the people who visit the museum (at least for the first time) don't want to miss the famous works of art.

No one wants to say that they visited the Louvre and didn't see the **Mona Lisa**.

The name of the artist who painted the Mona Lisa is Leonardo Da Vinci. An Italian nobleman ordered a portrait of his wife, whose name was Lisa Gherardini, from Da Vinci. The Mona Lisa is very famous, and it's said that there is a special secret in her smile.

Can you try to guess what the secret is?

Did you know?

It's said that in order to keep Lisa smiling until Leonardo finished painting her, he had an orchestra and clowns come to entertain her while he painted.

Most people want to be able to say that they saw the "Venus de Milo" statue.

It is one of the most famous statues of **Venus - the goddess of love** of the ancient Romans. She is considered to be the prettiest woman in the world. Many artists have tried to paint and sculpt her. Sadly, no one knows the identity of artist who made this famous statue.

And of course we can't pass-up on the
statue of the Sphinx

The statue of the **sphinx** is more than 4,000 years old. It shows Pharaoh with the body of a lion. In ancient Egypt they would put the sphinx at the entrance to temples because it was thought to be a symbol of protection and guardianship.

Here are some things that not everyone knows about the Louvre:

- The Louvre is the largest museum in the world
- The Louvre can host 20,000 visitors a day
- In 12 years the Louvre has hosted more visitors than the entire population of France
- For every French person who visits the Louvre there are two Americans...

And now to summarize your museum visits…
Museums Diary for the curious kid

So that we won't forget where we were and what we saw:

The name of the museums that we visited

_____

_____

_____

	Name of artwork	What material was used to make it, its size, colors and to which movement it belonged.	Where is it located? floor, wing, room?
1			
2			
3			
4			
5			
6			

Museum game - Find the work of art

Use the clues to find the work of art:

Each member of the family receives a piece of paper and a pen.

1. Each player picks a picture or statue and doesn't show it to the other players.

2. On the piece of paper, each player writes down (without the other players seeing) a description of the work that they chose – size, color, materials and other hints. (You're not allowed to write the name of the artist or of the work.)

3. Each player hands his or her paper to a different player.

4. Set a time limit (at least five minutes is recommended).

5. During this time, each player looks for the work described on his or her piece of paper.

6. When the time is up, each player returns the paper with the name of the artist and the work written on the other side.

7. Repeat for at least three more rounds.

8. The winner is the player who succeeds in identifying the largest number of works.

Good Luck!

The Museum of Science and Industry -
Parc de la Villette

This is one of the most important science museums in the country. The park is located in a pretty garden (as is fitting for beautiful Paris), and it has several areas and attractions. We'll recommend several that you shouldn't miss.

The City of Children and the City of Technology - Here you can experience all kinds of different exhibits: a TV studio, an auto assembly, robots and **computers**, the world of ants and more...Don't worry, even though the explanations are in French you can still have fun without understanding the language.

La Geode - The Silver Ball - Movies on different subjects are shown here every hour on a **giant screen.** It's said that this is the biggest screen in the world. When you buy your ticket at the entrance to the park you have to decide which movie you want to see. The movie is in French, but again, you don't have to understand the language to enjoy the movie that is shown on such a big and impressive screen ☺ .

Did you know?
The ball is constructed of 6433 triangles that are attached to each other with great precision.

The Planetarium - A spectacular show that tells about the earth and the solar system. It's important not to forget to reserve tickets ahead of time. You won't believe it, but 125 projectors project the show onto 32 screens…The narration is in French, but even if you don't know French you can still enjoy this unique experience.

The Submarine Argonaute - A real submarine that served in the French navy. Today it is a museum that allows you to see how the crew of the submarine lived.

Additional Attractions:

The Explora Centre - A section that contains booths exploring different types of topics such as transportation, pre-historic man and others.

City of Music - A beautiful, unique museum of musical instruments that is found in the southern part of the park. With a little luck maybe you'll be able to hear a nice concert. (With the park in the background the music is always prettier.)

Science City - Science and Industry Museum visit summary

So, where did we go? 😉

Do you remember all the places and installations that you visited in the Science and Industry Museum? So, where did you go?

- Did you visit the City of Children? Yes/No
  If so, what did you see there? What did you try out?

  _____

- Did you visit the Geode? Yes/No
  If so, which movie did you see?

  _____

- Did you see the show in the Planetarium? Yes/No

  _____

- Did you go into the submarine? Yes/No

  _____

- Did you go into the Explora exhibits (different theme areas)?
  Yes/No If so, which theme areas did you visit?

  _____

Family vote:
What was the **most interesting** thing you saw in the Science and Industry Museum?

First place _____

Second place _____

Third place _____

Museum Trivia

1. **What kind of art is found in the Musée Rodin?**
   a   Mostly bronze statues
   b   Huge murals
   c   A giant silver ball
   d   A range of abstract paintings

2. **In which building will you find the Musée D'Orsay?**
   a   In a beautiful building with a huge yard
   b   In a building that was once a train station
   c   In a building that was once a police station
   d   In a building with a huge glass pyramid at the entrance

3. **Who said, "Give me a museum and I'll fill it"?**
   a   Wassily Kandinsky
   b   Franz Marc
   c   Pablo Picasso
   d   Camille Pissarro

4. **In what style of art does the artist use small brushstrokes to paint things connected to his or her life?**
   a   Impressionism
   b   Expressionism
   c   Abstract art
   d   Portraiture

5. **In what style of art does the artist express his or her feelings and emotions?**
   a   Impressionism
   b   Expressionism
   c   Abstract art
   d   Portraiture

1a, 2b, 3c, 4a, 5b

6. If you see a painting in which the colors and shapes are undefined, you will know that the painting belongs to the school of:

a Impressionism
b Expressionism
c Abstract art
d Portraiture

7. If Leonardo wants to create a picture with colors that melt onto the page and look transparent, he will use:

a Gouache paint
b Water colors
c Oil paint
d Color pencils

8. In which museum will you find the famous statue, "Venus de Milo," of Venus, the goddess of Love?

a At the Musée D'Orsay
b At the Museum of Science and Industry
c At the Guggenheim Museum
d At the Louvre

9. Who painted the Mona Lisa, which is hanging in the Louvre?

a Wassily Kandinsky
b Marc Chagall
c Pablo Picasso
d Leonardo DaVinci

10. Auguste Rodin's most famous statue is called:

a The Indecisive One
b The Thinking Rodin
c The Greatest One
d The Thinker

6c, 7b, 8d, 9d, 10d

True or False:

1. The Louvre is the biggest museum in the world. True/False

2. There are paintbrushes made from horse tails. True/False

3. The statue of the Sphinx is considered to be a symbol of security and safekeeping in France. True/False

4. Most of the artwork in the Musée D'Orsay is from the school of Impressionism. True/False

5. A portrait is a landscape painting. True/False

6. Rodin created the statue called "The Thinker" several times. True/False

7. Usually, oil paints are used on rolls of paper. True/False

8. There are more than 100 museums in Paris. True/False

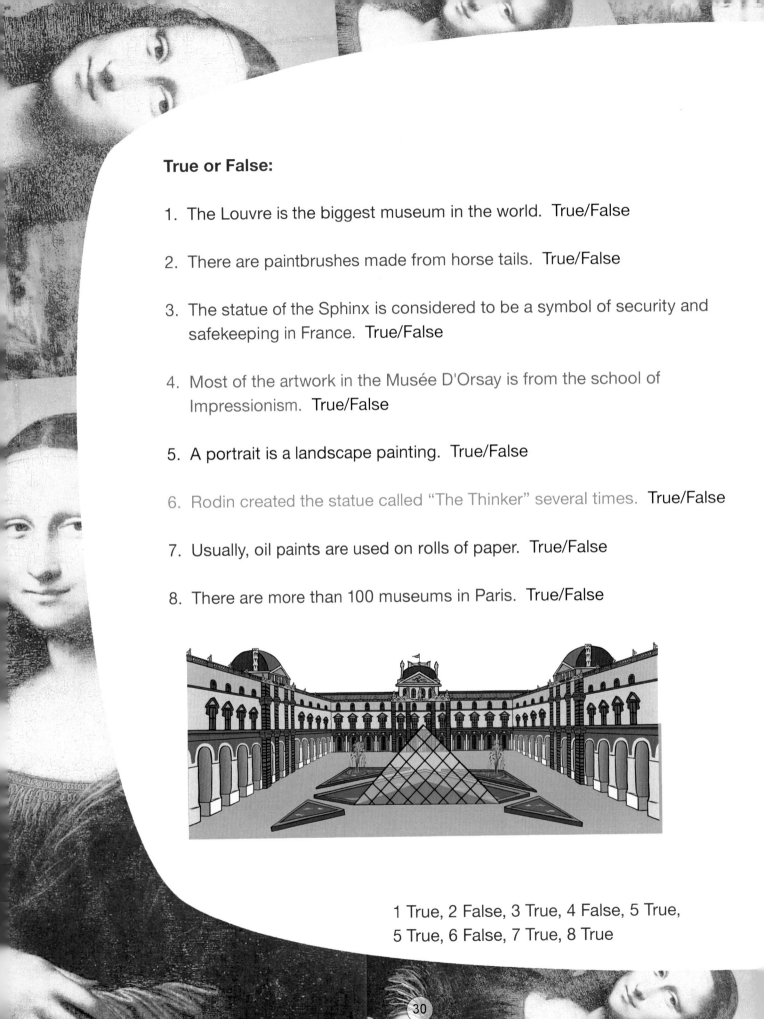

1 True, 2 False, 3 True, 4 False, 5 True,
5 True, 6 False, 7 True, 8 True

Made in United States
North Haven, CT
19 February 2024

48928789R10018